CELTIC SONGS
FOR THE
TENOR BANJO

37

*Traditional Songs and
Instrumentals*

from

*Ireland, Scotland, Wales, Cornwall,
Brittany, and the Isle of Man*

by Dick Sheridan

~oOo~
An exciting and diverse collection
of well-known favorites
and other choice selections

ISBN 978-1-57424-296-6
SAN 683-8022

Cover by James Creative Group

Banjo on cover - Orpheum Style #3, Serial # 9480
made in 1919 by Lange and Rettberg

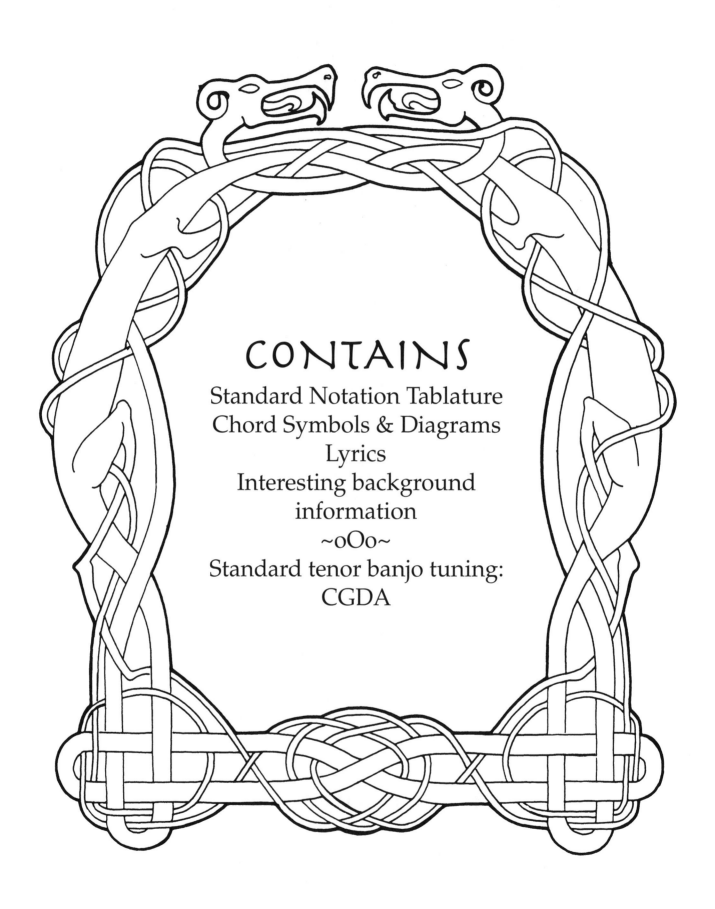

CONTAINS

Standard Notation Tablature
Chord Symbols & Diagrams
Lyrics
Interesting background
information
~oOo~
Standard tenor banjo tuning:
CGDA

TABLE OF CONTENTS

Song types and typical time signatures
Jigs and Double jigs - 6/8
Slip jigs - 9/8
Reels and Marches - 4/4
Hornpipes - 2/4 and 4/4
Waltzes - 3/4
Airs - 2/4, 3/4. 4/4. 6/8

ABOUT THE AUTHOR

Dick Sheridan's introduction to the tenor banjo came during his early college years. Dixieland jazz was going through a major revival, and the campus jazz band needed a banjo player. Because Dick played ukulele and guitar, he was recruited; a small banjo-mandolin was located and tuned like a ukulele.

Soon after in an antique shop, Dick spotted a banjo case hidden away under a table. The brown leatherette case appeared brand new and so did the banjo it contained – a Lyric tenor banjo manufactured by the Bacon Banjo Company of Groton, Connecticut. Dick was euphoric. He didn't have a real banjo – nor did he have the asking price of $35. Fast as he could, he hurried home to ask his father to underwrite the instrument. His dad agreed, the banjo was purchased, and it still remains a treasured possession to this day.

Initially the Lyric banjo was tuned like a ukulele, but it wasn't long before the urge came to learn a proper banjo tuning. A few lessons and a pile of method books made the transition, and a lifelong dedication to tenor tuning resulted.

Following college, Dick continued to play the banjo, this time with another Dixieland group that has now been in existence for over 40 years. Concurrently he joined an Irish band, and it was then that his love of traditional Celtic music developed.

Dick claims that during the preparation of this book --and long after -- his head was spinning with the echoes of these haunting Celtic melodies with their lilting rhythms and unique harmonies. He feels sure you'll find the same experience as you discover the fun, enjoyment, and years of pleasure that await you and your tenor banjo in the following pages.

INTRODUCTION

Tweeds, tartans, and kilts; echoes of skirling bagpipes and the beat of the Irish bodhrán drum; cloud-covered highlands; misty moors and glens; the smell of burning peat and the surging surf along the jagged coasts of the Irish Sea and pounding Atlantic. The images are Celtic, and they're all reflected in the treasury of iconic music that now awaits you and your tenor banjo in the following pages.

Who were these Celts who have left us such an incredibly legacy of culture, language, religion, and musical heritage? History shows them to have been a group of tribal societies pre-dating the Christian era by many hundreds of years. They ranged across central Europe and the Iberian (Spanish) peninsula, moving on to what is now Great Britain, Ireland, and western France.

The principal traces of their diaspora are now concentrated in the six Celtic "nations" of Ireland and Scotland – Cornwall and Wales on the west coast of England – the Isle of Man in the Irish Sea – and Brittany (Bretagne in French) across from Cornwall on the northwest coast of France.

It is noteworthy that in the midst of English and French speaking countries, traces of early Celtic languages can still be heard and many are learning and speaking it fluently. Remnants survive in Irish and Scottish "Gaelic," and lingering examples can be found in the other nations, but native speakers are few. Attempts are currently being made to revive these ancient languages along with a renewed interest in Celtic music and the arts. Festivals are flourishing, and much attention is being directed to the old songs and dances. Traditional instruments are being resurrected, while newer ones – like the tenor banjo – are being added

One especially well-known festival is in the village of Helston in south Cornwall. Called the "Furry Day Festival" it pays homage in early May to the arrival of spring. (The term "furry" is considered to be a corruption of the Middle English or Latin words for "celebration" or "festivity.") Parades, pageants, concerts, and dances highlight the event, and long lines of merrymakers march the village streets weaving in and out of houses and shops, in one door and out another, wherever their wanderings should take them.

It should be mentioned that The "Furry Day Carol" included in this collection is not a Christmas carol but rather one linked – like the Furry Day Festival itself – to the celebration of the passing of winter and the onset of spring.

Another event in Cornwall that is enjoying a resurgence of interest is an old "West Country" custom of England called "Crying The Neck." It occurs in early September at the end of the harvest season. The last-standing sheaf of corn or wheat is cut, held high for onlookers, with the chanting of an ancient rhyme or song that was traditionally sung by reapers. The sheaf is taken to a nearby village church where a brief service is held followed by a supper of cakes and pasties. A "corn dolly" is made from the sheaf and then hung in the church as a symbol of hope for a bountiful harvest the following year. All this occurs at the time of "harvest home" when crops are finally gathered and brought in from the fields with much ceremony and celebration. (See the tune "Harvest Home" included in this collection.)

Celtic jigs and reels, old airs and quaint dances, stem from the folk traditions of Western Europe. Even our own culture acknowledges a Celtic contribution with the holiday favorites of "Deck The Hall" from Wales and "Auld Lang Syne" from Scotland. Moreover, it is thought that "The First Nowell" has its origin in Cornwall.

The migration of Celts from Cornwall across the Atlantic Ocean to Brittany has produced an anomaly of cultures and traditions in France, not unlike that of Québec in Canada. Festivals and carnivals with Celtic roots abound, like the Fest Noz and religious processions called "Pardons." In the Breton city of Quimper there's a "Festival of Cornouaille," and it seems reasonable to assume that the name reflects the exodus of Celts from Cornwall.

Indeed, Celtic music thrives today as evidenced by folk revivals, recordings, concert hall performances, and the growing number of enthusiasts throughout the world. Lively, spirited, haunting, quaint, nostalgic – all of these terms apply, and the music is as current today as it was centuries ago.

It's your turn now to join the fun and share the excitement. "Céad Míle Fáilte". That's an Irish greeting which means "A hundred thousand welcomes." By extension the welcome extends to you from all six nations inviting you to sample the treasury of wonderful music that's in store for you and your tenor banjo in the pages that follow.

ALL THROUGH THE NIGHT

Tenor Banjo: CGDA

Traditional Welsh

AN ALARC'H

Tenor banjo: CGDA

Traditional Breton

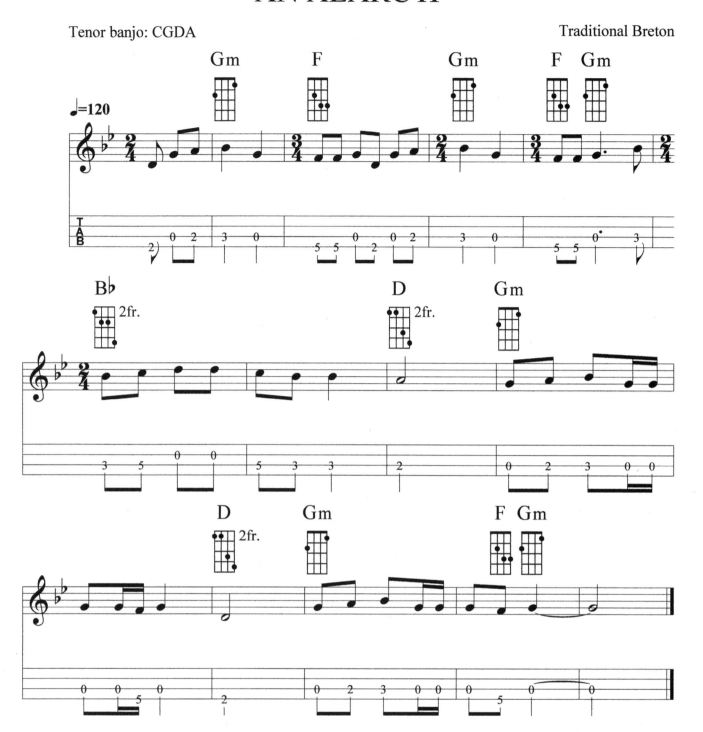

ARRANE ASHOONAGH DY VANNIN

The National Anthem of the Isle of Man

JOHN J. KNEEN

Tenor banjo: CGDA

WILLIAM HENRY GILL

THE ASH GROVE

Tenor Banjo: CGDA

JOHN OXENFORD, verse 1
THOMAS OLIPHANT, verse 2

Traditional Welsh

1.Down yon - der green val - ley where stream-lets me - an - der, when
at the bright noon-tide in sol - i - tude wan - der, a -

twi - light is__ fad - ing, I pen - sive - ly rove. Or
mid the__ dark shades of the lone - ly ash_____ grove. 'Twas

there while__ the__ black - bird was cheer - ful - ly__ sing - ing, I

10

THE ASH GROVE

2. Still glows the bright sunshine o'er valley and mountains,
   Still warbles the blackbird its note from the tree;
   Still trembles the moonbeam on streamlet and fountains,
   But what are the beauties of nature to me?
   With sorrow, deep sorrow, my bosom is laden,
   All day I go mourning in search of my love;
   Ye echoes, oh, tell me, where is the sweet maiden?
   "She sleeps 'neath the green turf down by the ash grove."

BLACKBIRD WILL YOU GO?

Tenor Banjo: CGDA

Traditional Welsh

BLUEBELLS OF SCOTLAND

Tenor Banjo: CGDA

Traditional Scottish

O where and O where does your highland laddie dwell?
O where and O where does your highland laddie dwell?
He dwells in merry Scotland where blooms the sweet bluebell,
And it's all in my heart that I love my laddie well.

THE CAMPBELLS ARE COMING

Tenor banjo: CGDA

Traditional Scottish

CHORUS

VERSE: Great Argyll goes before, before,
He makes the cannons and guns to roar,
Wi' sound of trumpet, pipe and drum,
The Campbells are coming, o-ho, o-ho.

CHORUS

~oOo~

CHORUS

VERSE: The Campbells they are a' in arms,
Their loyal faith and truth to show,
Wi' banners rattling in the wind ,
The Campells are coming, o-ho, o-ho.

CHORUS

COMIN' THRO' THE RYE

ROBERT BURNS   Tradional Scottish Melody

DANS LÉON

With appreciation to John and Sondra Bromka of Bells & Motley for this beautiful transcription.

Tenor banjo: CGDA

Traditional Breton

CORNISH WASSAIL

Tenor banjo: CGDA

Traditional

♩=130

Now Christ - mas is com - en and New Year be - gin, pray

o - pen your doors and let us come in. With

our was - sail, was - sail, was - sail, and

joy come with our jol - ly wa - sail.

CORNISH WASSAIL

At Christmas time the ancient tradition of wassailing still exists in some rural areas of Ireland and Great Britain. Small groups go from house to house good-naturedly begging some token of holiday remembrance -- a few coins, some fruit or pastry, or more usually libation from the wassail bowl. Other wassails with different melodies from the "Cornish Wassail" but with similar lyrics can be found in Centerstream's *Yultide Favorites For Ukulele."*

O master and mistress sitting down by the fire,
While we poor wassailers do travel the mire.
With our wassail ... etc.

Good master, good mistress, sitting down at your ease,
Put your hand in your pocket and give what you please.
With our wassail ... etc.

We come to this place and orderly stand,
We're jolly wassailers with bowl in our hand.
With our wassail ... etc.

We hope that your barley will prosper and grow
That you may have plenty and some to bestow.
With our wassail ... etc.

We hope that your apple trees prosper and bear,
And bring forth good cider when we come next year.
With our wassail ... etc.

We wish you great plenty and a long time to live
Since you've been so willing and freely to give.
With our wassail ... etc.

DROWSY MAGGIE

Tenor Banjo: CGDA

Traditional Irish Reel

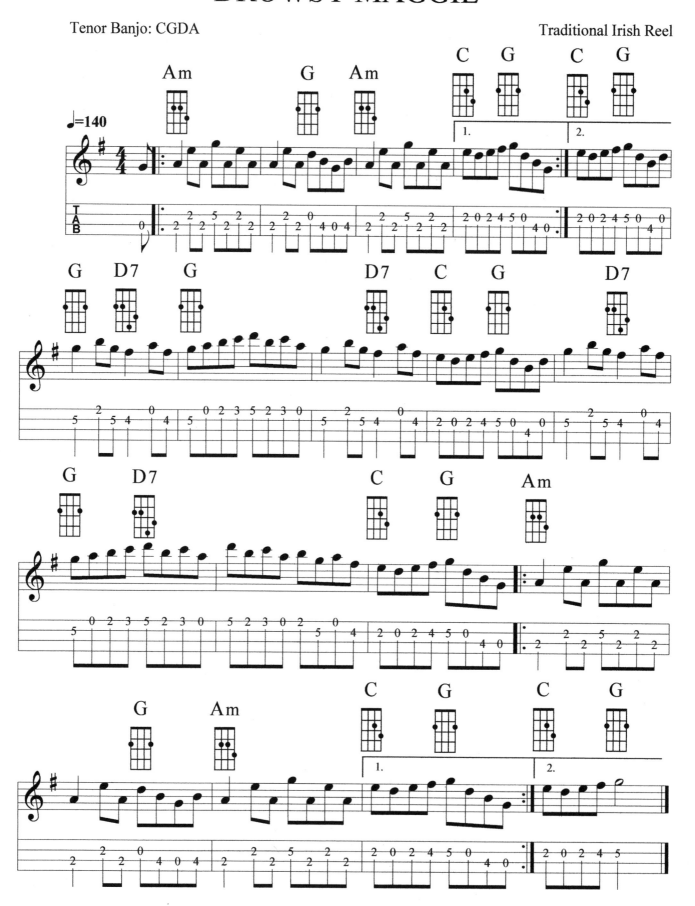

FAREWELL TO WHISKEY

(Ladies' Triumph)

Tenor Banjo: CGDA

Traditional

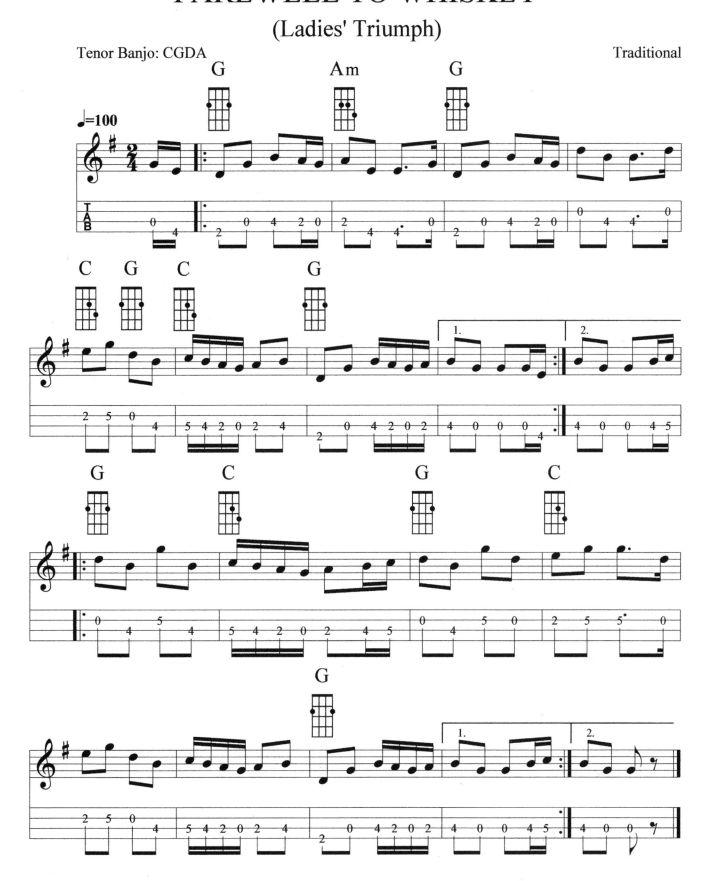

FLOW GENTLY, SWEET AFTON

Tenor Banjo: CGDA

ROBERT BURNS

JONATHAN E. SPILMAN

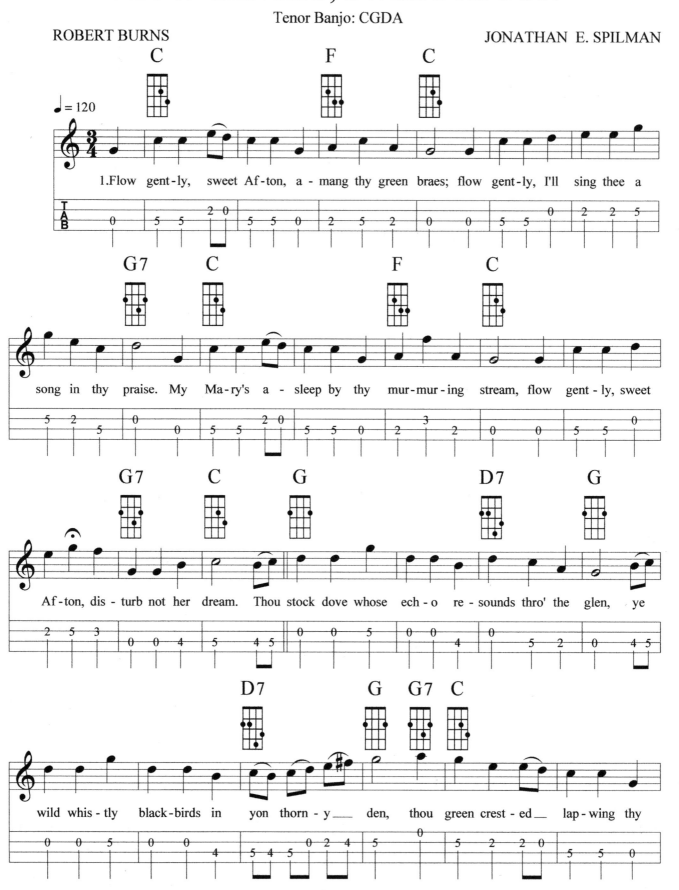

scream-ing for - bear, I charge you, dis - turb not my slum - ber - ing fair.

2. How lofty, sweet Afton, thy neighboring hills,
   Far marked with the courses of clear winding rills!
   There daily I wander, as morn rises high,
   My flocks and my Mary's sweet cot in my eye.
      How pleasant thy banks and green valleys below,
      Where wild in the woodlands the primroses blow!
      There oft as mild evening creeps over the lea,
      The sweet-scented birk shades my Mary and me.

3. Thy crystal stream, Afton, how lovely it glides,
   And winds by the cot where my Mary resides!
   How wonton thy waters her snowy feet lave,
   As, gath'ring sweet flow'rets, she stems thy clear wave.
      Flow gently, sweet Afton, amang thy green braes,
      Flow gently, sweet river, the theme of my lays:
      My Mary's asleep by thy murmuring stream,
      Flow gently, sweet Afton, disturb not her dream.

NOTE: The melody of "Flow Gently, Sweet Afton" is often heard as a variant for the Christmas carol "Away In A Manger."

FURRY DAY CAROL

Tenor Banjo: CGDA

Traditional Cornish

THE GALWAY PIPER

Tenor banjo: CGDA

Traditional Irish

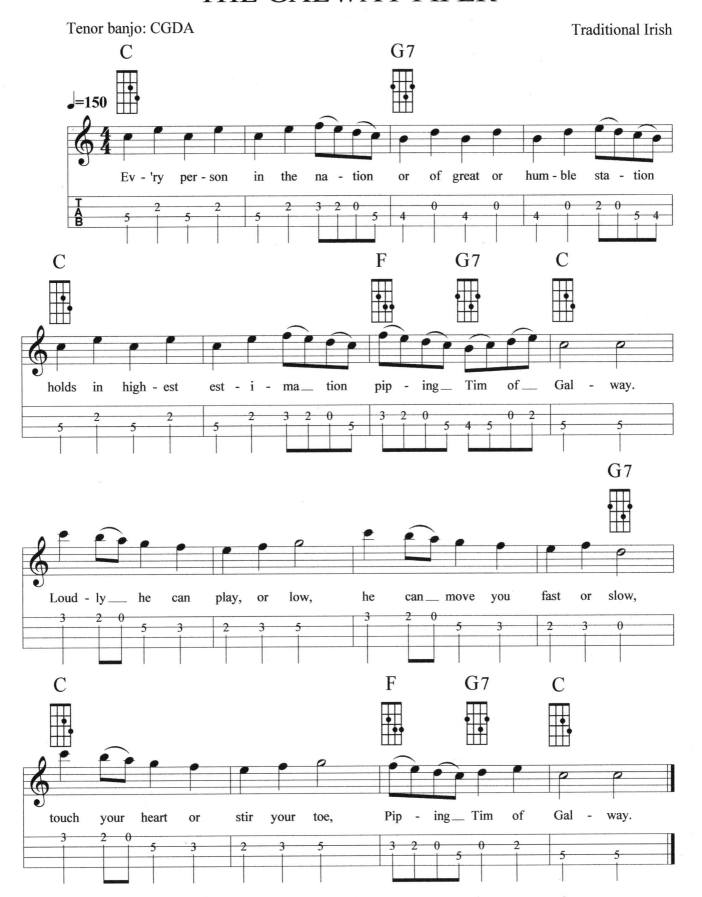

GARRY OWEN

Tenor Banjo: CGDA

Traditional Irish Double Jig

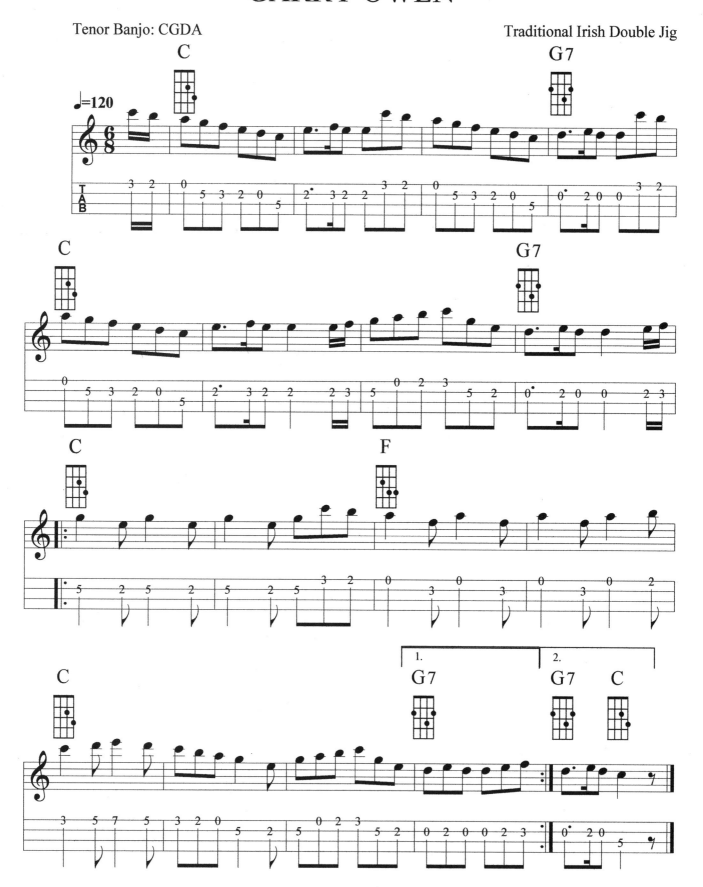

HARVEST HOME

Tenor Banjo: CGDA

Traditional Hornpipe

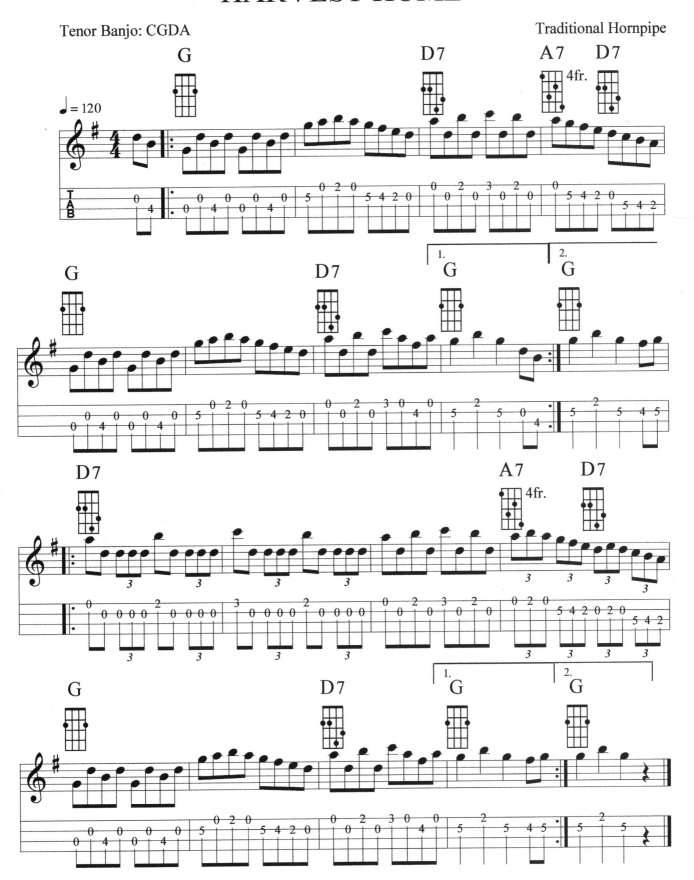

HASTE TO THE WEDDING

Tenor Banjo: CGDA

Traditional Irish

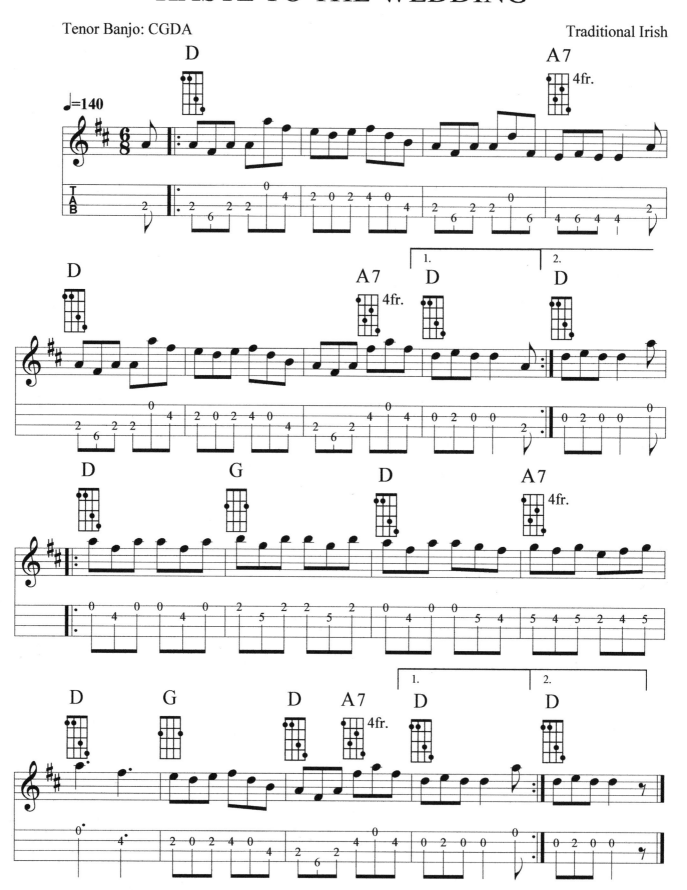

IRISH WASHERWOMAN

Tenor Banjo: CGDA

Traditional Irish Jig

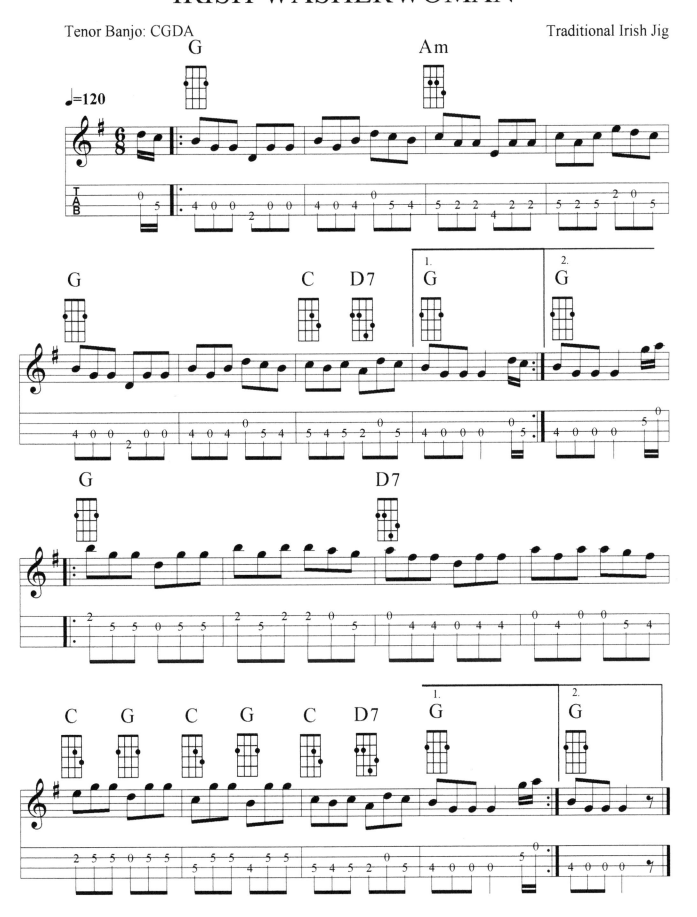

HELSTON FURRY DANCE

Tenor banjo: CGDA

Traditional Cornish

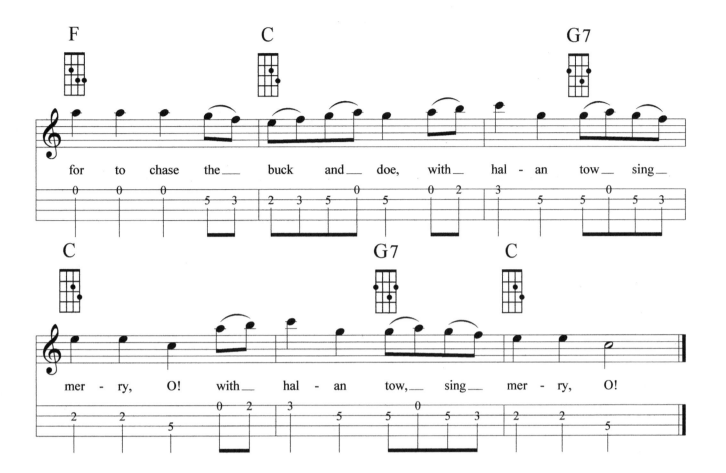

F   C   G7

for   to   chase   the __ buck   and __ doe,   with __ hal - an   tow __ sing __

C   G7   C

mer - ry,   O!   with __ hal - an   tow, __ sing __ mer - ry,   O!

2. Saint George next will be our song,
   Saint George he was a knight, O!
   Of all the kings in Christendom
   King Georgy is the right, O!
   In ev'ry land where'er we go,
   Sing halan tow and George, O!
   Sing halan tow and George, O!

3. God bless Aunt Mary Moses*
   And all her powers and might, O!
   And send us peace in merry England,
   Both day and night, O!
   Pray send us peace both day and night
   With halan tow, sing merry, O!
   With halan tow, sing merry, O!.

* Aunt: a term of respect
  Moses: a corrupted old Cornish word for "maid"
  Hence, a reference to Maid Mary, the Vigin Mary

The "Helston Furry Dance" with slight variations is known by such names as "The Helstone Foray," "The Furry Day Song," and "The Floral Dance," among others. Note the similarity with this song and "The Furry Day Carol" also included in this collection.

THE KERRY DANCE

Tenor banjo: CGDA

JAMES LYNAM MOLLOY

THE KERRY DANCE

KING OF THE FAIRIES

Tenor Banjo: CGDA

Traditional

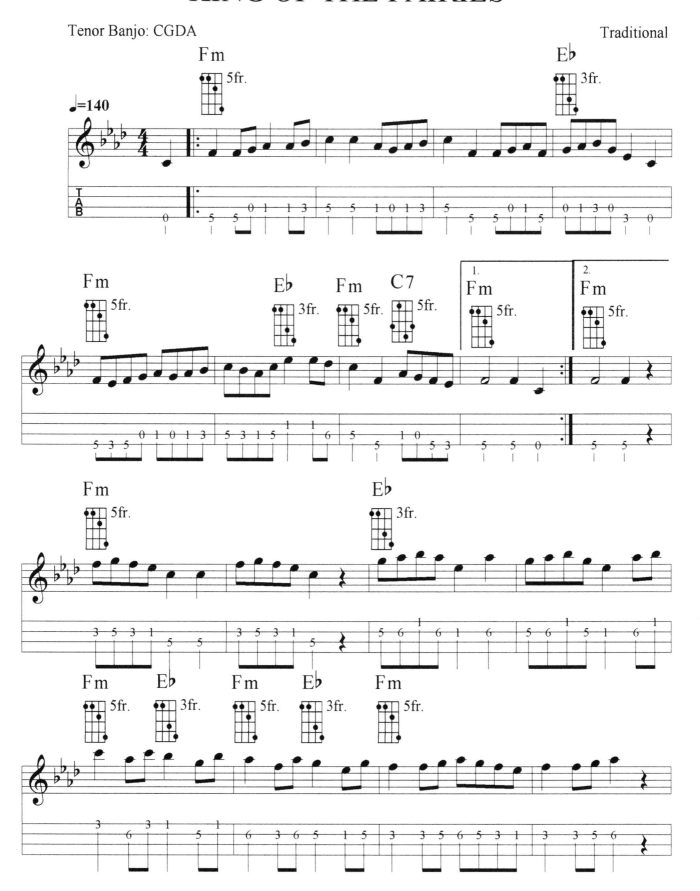

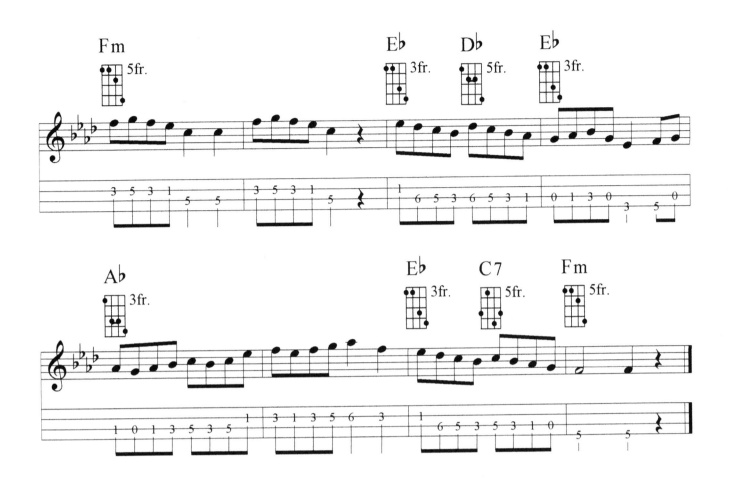

LOCH LOMOND

Tenor Banjo: CGDA

Traditional Scottish

MASON'S APRON

Tenor Banjo: CGDA

Traditional

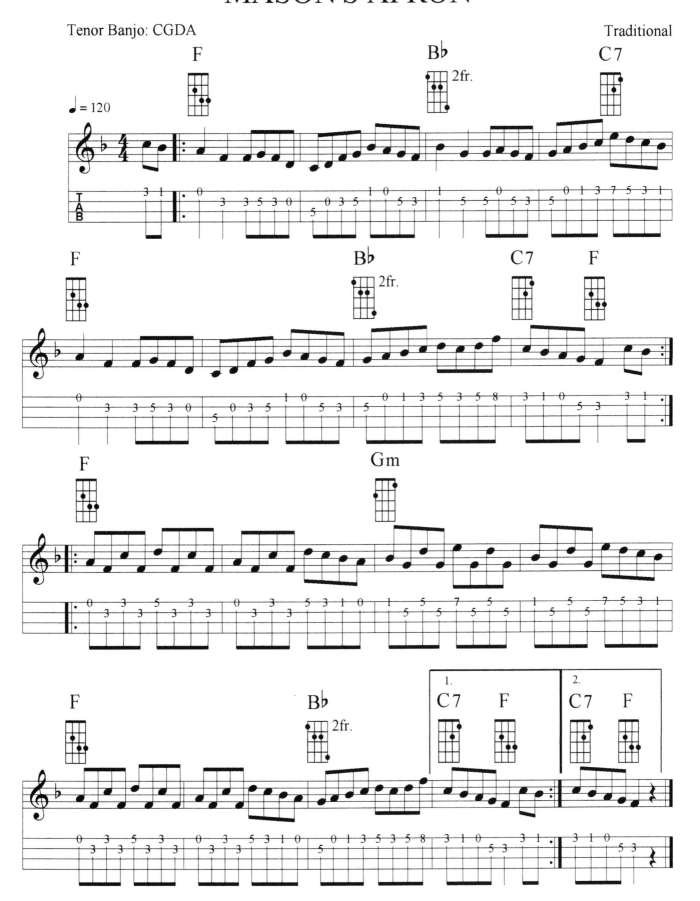

MEN OF HARLECH

Tenor banjo: CGDA

JOHN OXENFORD (1873)

Traditional Welsh

1. Men of Har - lech, march to glo - ry, vic - to - ry is hov' - 'ring o'er ye,
2. At your sloth she seems to won - der; rend the slug - gish bonds a - sun - der,

bright - eyed free - dom stands be - fore ye, hear ye not her call?
let the war - cry's deaf - 'ning thun - der ev - 'ry foe ap - pall.

Ech - oes loud - ly wak - ing; hill and val - ley shak - ing;

'till the sound spreads wide a - round, the Sax - on's cour - age break - ing;

MEN OF HARLECH

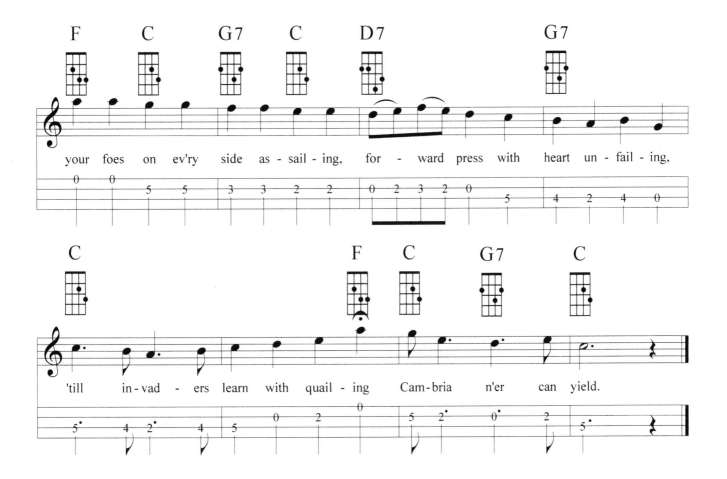

your foes on ev'ry side as - sail - ing, for - ward press with heart un - fail - ing, 'till in - vad - ers learn with quail - ing Cam - bria n'er can yield.

Numerous variants can be found for the lyrics of this popular regimental march. The song commemorates the seven-year siege of Harlech Castle in Wales (1461 to 1468) by the forces of Edward IV who reigned from 1461 to 1483. Ruins of the castle still exist and are open to the public. The castle sits high atop a rocky promontory overlooking the Irish Sea.

MUCKIN' O' GEORDIE'S BYRE

Tenor banjo: CGDA

Traditional Scottish

MUCKIN' O' GEORDIE'S BYRE

The comical words of this lilting song bewail the series of misfortunes attending
Geordie MacIntyre, his wife and daughter while trying to clean up their long-neglected
barn. The Scottish dialect of the lyrics is far too challenging for the uninitiated, a sample
of which is given below, along with an attempt at translation. Check the Internet
"Songs Of Scotland" for the full set of words.

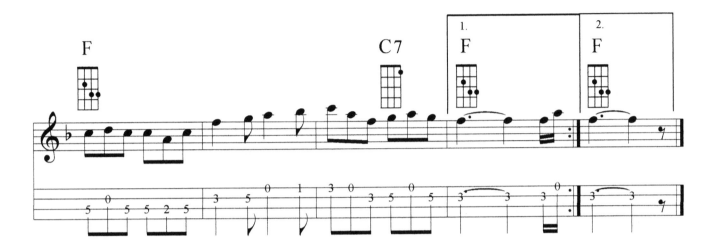

At a relic aul' croft upon the hill,
Roon the neuk frae Sprottie's mill,
Tryin' a' his life tae jine the kill
Lived Geordie MacIntyre.

He had a wife a swir's himsel',
An' a daughter as black's auld Nick himsel,
There was some fun-haud awa' the smell
At the muckin' o' Geordie's byre.

For the grain was tint, the besome was deen,
The barra widna row its leen,
An' siccan a soss it never was seen
At the muckin' o' Geordie's byre.

For the daughter had to strae and neep,
The auld wife started to sweep the greep,
When Geordie fell sklite on a rotten heap
At the muckin' of Geordie's byre.
Etc.

At an old cottage upon the hill,
Round the bend from Sprottie's mill,
Trying all his life to overcome laziness
Lived Geordie MacIntyre.

He had a wife as unwilling to work as himself,
And a daughter as bad as the Devil,
Some fun was had along with the smell
At the cleaning of Geordie's barn.

For the grain was lost, the broom was done,
The barrow wouldn't hold its load,
And such a dirty mess was never seen
At the cleaning of Gorordie's barn.

For the daughter had to straw and feed the cattle,
The old wife started to sweep the gutter,
When Geordie fell heavily on a rotten heap
At the cleaning of Geordie's barn.
Etc.

MISS McLEOD'S REEL

Tenor banjo: CGDA

Traditional Scottish & Irish

O'GALLAGHER'S FROLICS

Tenor Banjo: CGDA

Traditional Irish

PLANXTY IRWIN

Tenor Banjo: CGDA

Traditional Irish

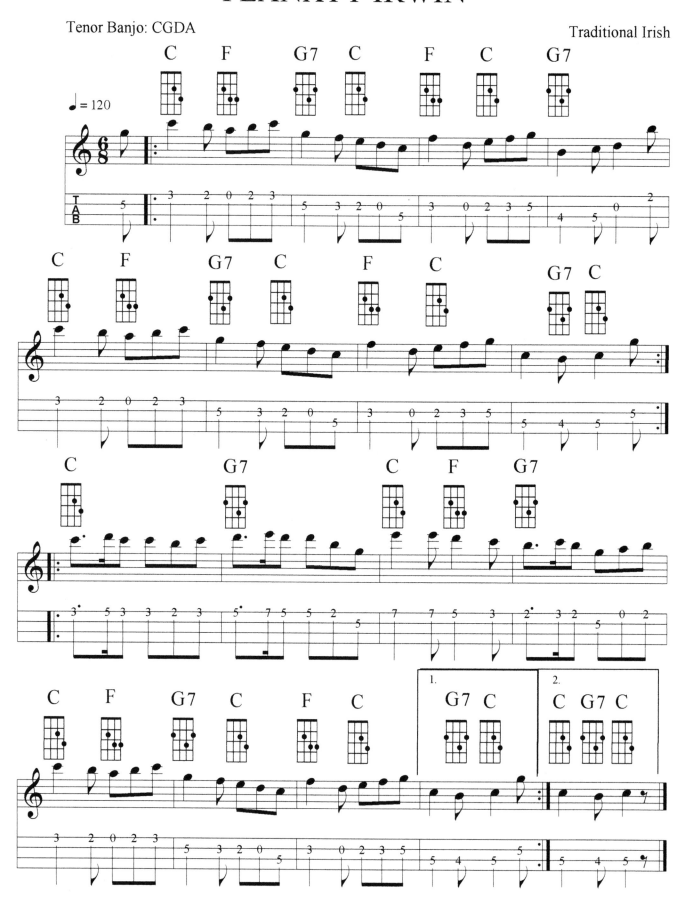

RED HAIRED BOY

Tenor banjo: CGDA

Traditional Irish

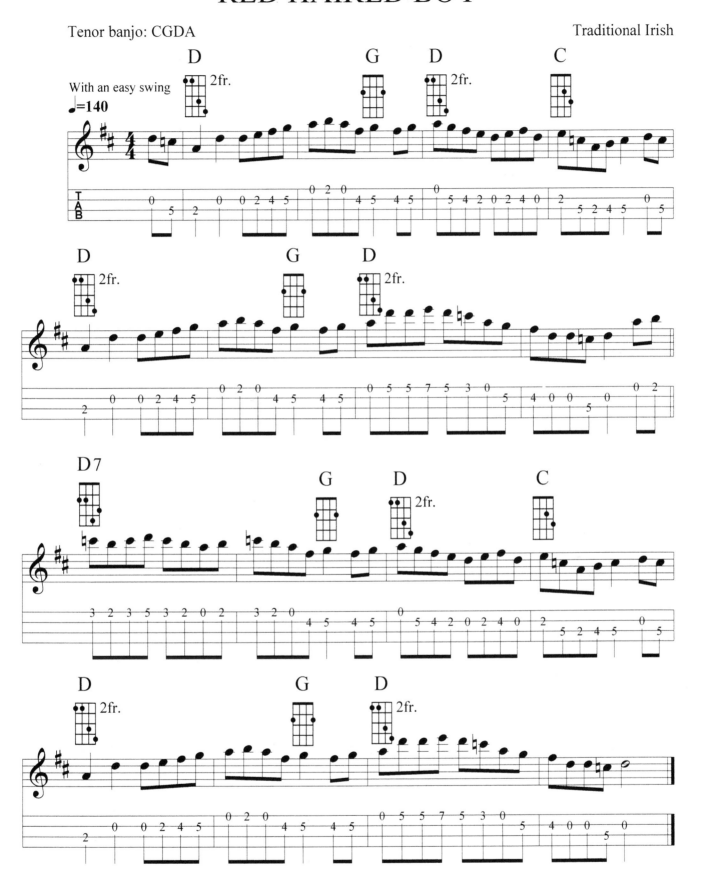

RICKETT'S HORNPIPE

(Manchester Hornpipe)

Tenor Banjo: CGDA

Traditional Scottish

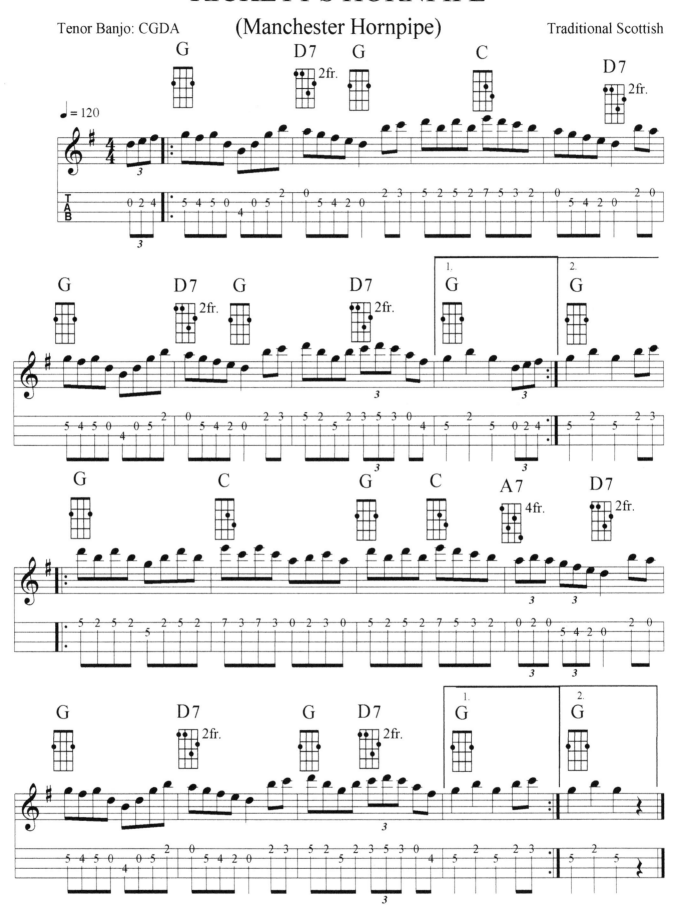

SADDLE THE PONY
(The Red Stocking)

Tenor Banjo: CGDA

Traditional

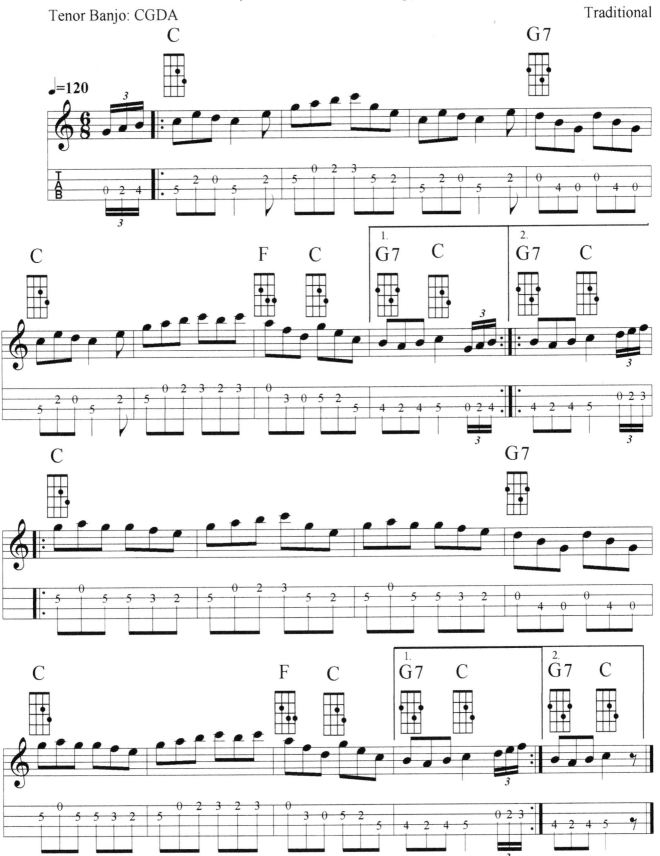

SKYE BOAT SONG

Tenor Banjo: CGDA

Traditional Scottish

2. Tho the waves leap, soft shall ye sleep,
   Ocean's a royal bed;
   Rocked in the deep, Flora* will keep
   Watch by your weary head.
   Chorus

3. Many's the lad fought on that day,
   Well claymore** could wield;
   When night came, silently lay
   Dead on Culloden's field.
   Chorus

4. Burn'd are our homes, exile and death
   Scatter'd our loyal men;
   Yet, e'er the sword cool in the sheath,
   Charlie will come again.
   Chorus

* Flora -- Flora MacDonald, disguised Prince Charles as her maidservant thereby
aiding his escape.

** Claymore -- A broad doubled-edged sword favored by Scottish Highlanders.

Note: The Battle of Culloden Moors in 1756 pitted Prince Charles Edward Stuart ("Bonnie Prince Charlie") and his clans of Highlanders against the Duke of Cumberland in an attempt to regain the British throne and re-seat the House of Stuart. Charles was defeated and escaped to the Isle of Skye, situated in the Inner Hebrides off the west coast of Scotland.

STAR OF THE COUNTY DOWN

Tenor banjo: CGDA

Traditional Irish

2. She looked so sweet from her two bare feet,
   To the sheen of her nut-brown hair,
   Such a coaxing elf, sure I shook myself,
   For to see I was really there.
      Chorus

3. As she onward sped, sure I scratched my head,
   And I looked with a feeling rare,
   And I says, says I, to a passer-by,
   "Who's the maid with the nut-brown hair?"
      Chorus

4. He smiled at me and he says, says he,
   "That's the gem of Ireland's crown,
   Young Rosie McCann from the banks of the Bann,
   She's the star of the County Down."
      Chorus

5. At the harvest fair, she'll be surely there,
   So I dress in my Sunday clothes,
   With my shoes shone bright and my hat cocked right,
   For a smile from my nut-brown rose.
      Chorus

6. No pipe I'll smoke, no horse I'll yoke,
   Till my plow is a rust-colored brown,
   Till a smiling bride by my own fireside,
   Sits the star of the County Down.
      Chorus

SWALLOW TAIL JIG

Tenor Banjo: CGDA

Traditional Irish

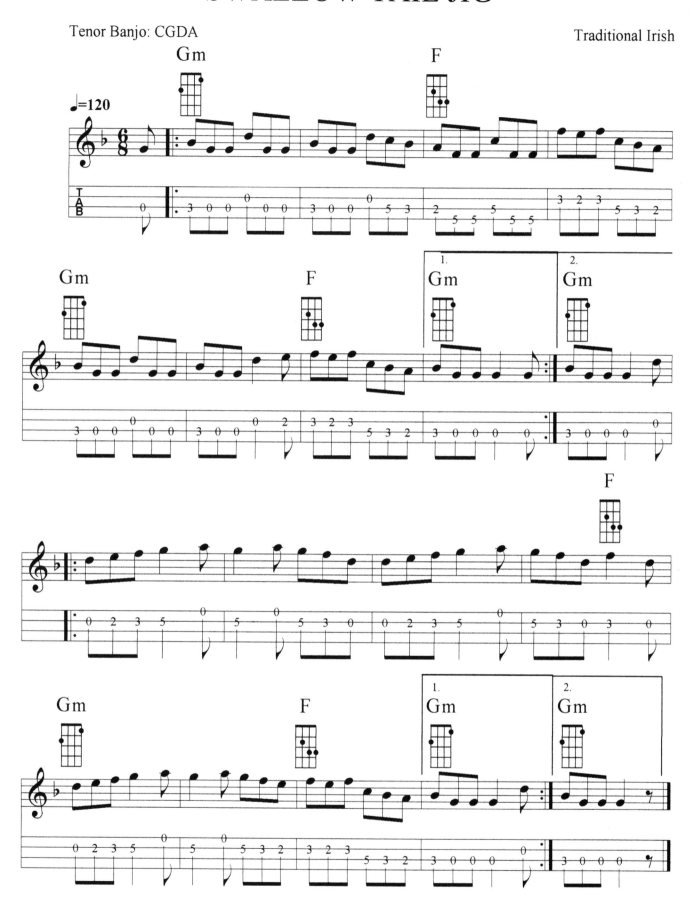

SCOTLAND THE BRAVE

Tenor banjo: CGDA

Traditional

TRIPPING UP THE STAIRS

Tenor Banjo: CGDA

Traditional Irish

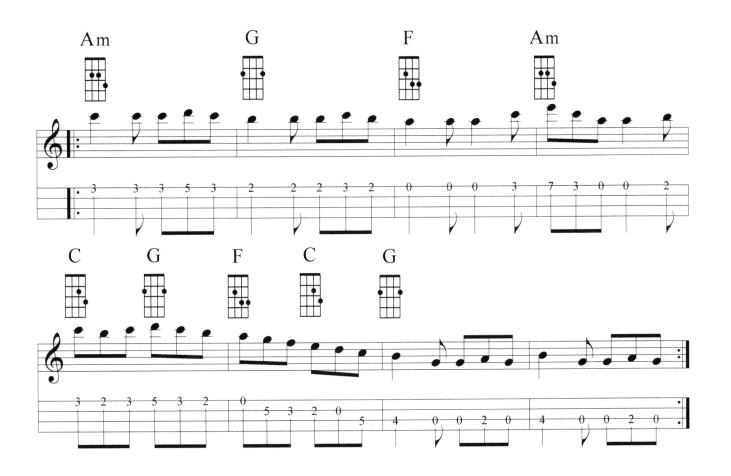

INDEX - SONGS BY NATION

Visit our Centerstream website at www.centerstream-usa.com for a complete list of publications for a variety of instruments plus instructional, reference books, biographies and DVDs.

56